Rhymes from the Reef

Kathy Bjornestad

Beartown
Press

Reviews

Rhymes from the Reef *is a collection of well-written, educational, and entertaining poems, enhanced by exceptional photography and illustrations. It is a treasure for any reader.*

-Eugene M. Gagliano, Wyoming Poet Laureate/Children's Author

With valiant verse, fascinating facts, and photographs that both suck you in and make you yearn for your own Caribbean vacation, this delightful book will be engaging for readers of all ages. I cannot wait to have copies of this masterpiece in all of my school libraries!

-Jennisen Lucas, District Librarian and Past President of AASL (American Association of School Librarians)

Dedications

To my mother, Janet, who put books in my hands before I could speak, and who let me out of chores if I had pen and paper in hand.

-Kathy Bjornestad

To Wave Runner and Beach Zombie—never stop exploring the world outside your world!

-Heidi Stefanich

A Note About the Real Pirates of the Caribbean

Rhymes from the Reef makes several references to pirates. During the Golden Age of Piracy (1600s -1700s), famous pirates like Blackbeard ruled the Caribbean Sea. These pirates (sometimes called swabbies) fought each other and the English navy. They endured fierce storms. Sometimes their ships sank, leaving underwater wrecks for treasure hunters to find hundreds of years later. Pirates who drowned were said to have gone to "Davy Jones' Locker." Some of the sea creatures in this book may have swum through ruined schooners and among chests of golden coins.

• • ● ● ● • ● ● ● • •

Where this Book's Photos were Taken

When *Rhymes from the Reef* photographer Heidi Stefanich visited the U.S. Virgin Islands of St. Thomas and St. John, she spent many hours each day snorkeling and captured amazing underwater sea life on her digital camera. Later, she recommended this vacation spot to the author, Kathy Bjornestad. The fragile beauty of the Virgin Islands inspired Bjornestad to write poetry about the vanishing reef.

The United States Virgin Islands are a U.S. territory located southeast of Florida and just east of Puerto Rico. They include three islands: St. Croix, St. Thomas, and St. John. The islands are world-famous for their crystal-clear waters and white sand beaches. Most of the photos in this book were captured in the waters off St. Thomas and St. John.

Under the Sea

Near the lollipop forests

and mangrove meadows

of the southern Caribbean Sea

live loads of creatures

with colorful features—

a world of diversity.

When you dive off the coasts

of white sand beaches

where wild Sargassum grows,

you'll see rainbow hues,

enjoy vivid views—

a landscape very few know.

Here in the coral

and under the surf

live lobsters and clownfish and eels,

so foreign and strange

in their undersea range,

you'd hardly believe they were real.

Tarpon

For years untold
I've shared this land
with Stegosaurs
and raptor bands.
At eight feet long,
my strength's unmatched.
Torpedo fast—
I'm hard to catch.

I arrow up
to gulp in air,
then slice a wave,
go back down where
the shrimp and crabs
and lobsters creep,
a yummy picnic
in the deep.

Fun Fact

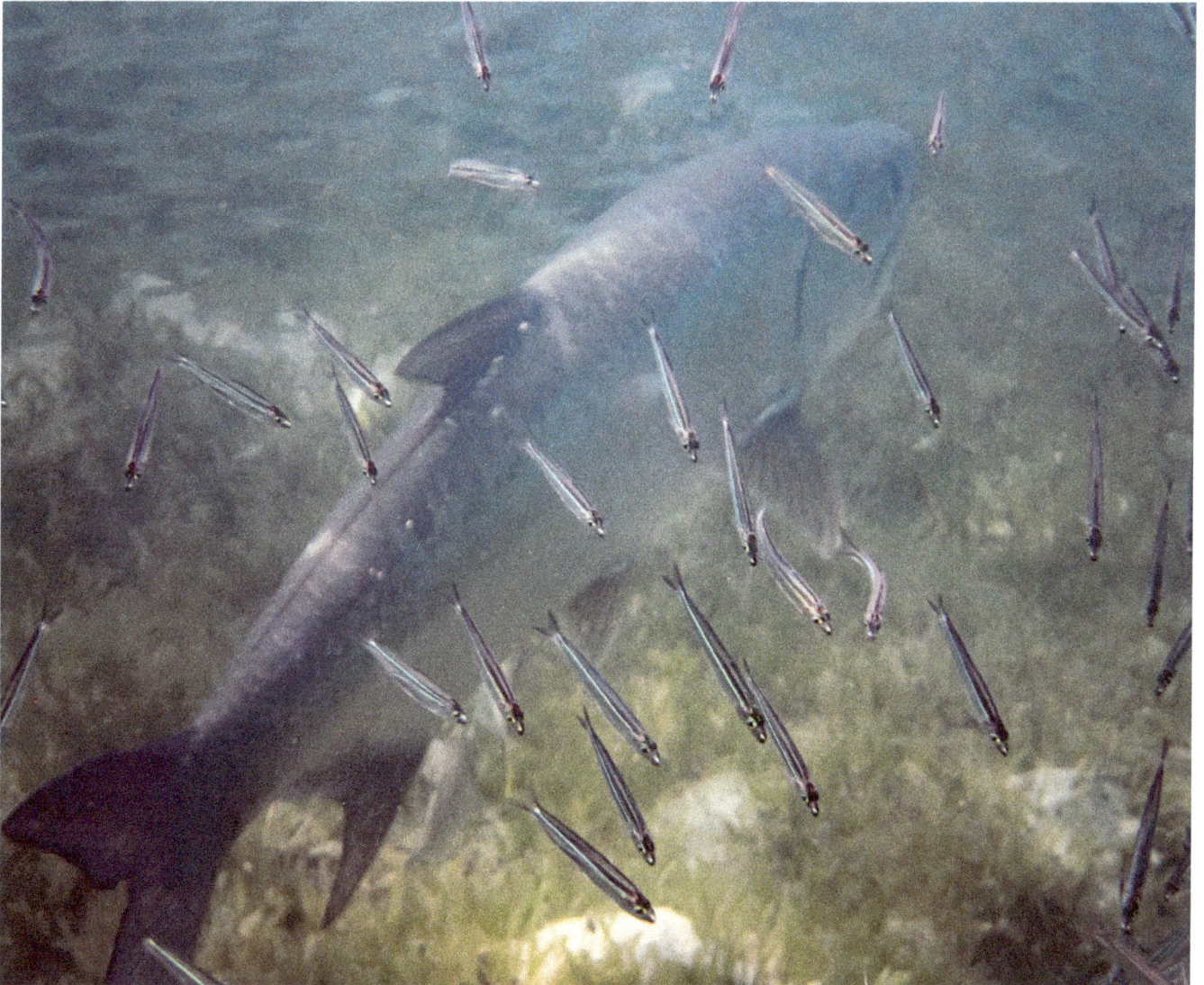

Tarpon, nicknamed "silver kings," can live over 50 years.

Damselfish

Do not be deceived, we're not

the sort of damsels that you thought.

Damsels in distress? Oh no!

We love to fight like wrestling pros!

Our size and clownish colors make

you think you'd like us in your tank,

but we are fighters from the reef,

plentiful and full of teeth!

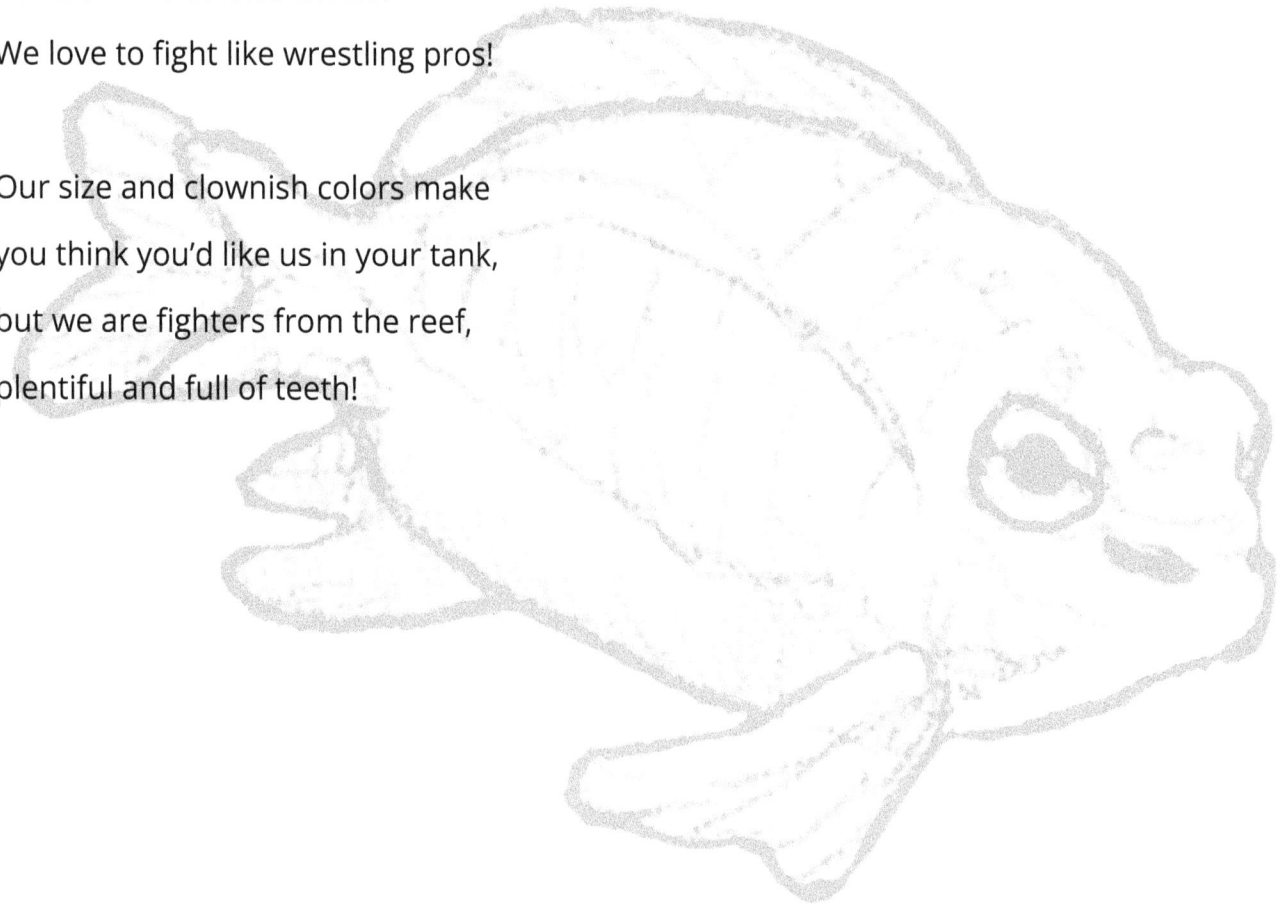

Fun Fact

There are approximately 315 species of damselfish. They aggressively guard their territory with very sharp teeth.

Jellyfish

Mushroom-headed

Brainless

Eyeless

Squirting water from its mouth.

Flailing

Stinging

Bell-shaped warning

Waving tentacles about.

Ghostly

Silent, deadly

Wondrous

Constant of the seas.

Pulsing

Pulling

Graceful drifter

Marvel of the deep.

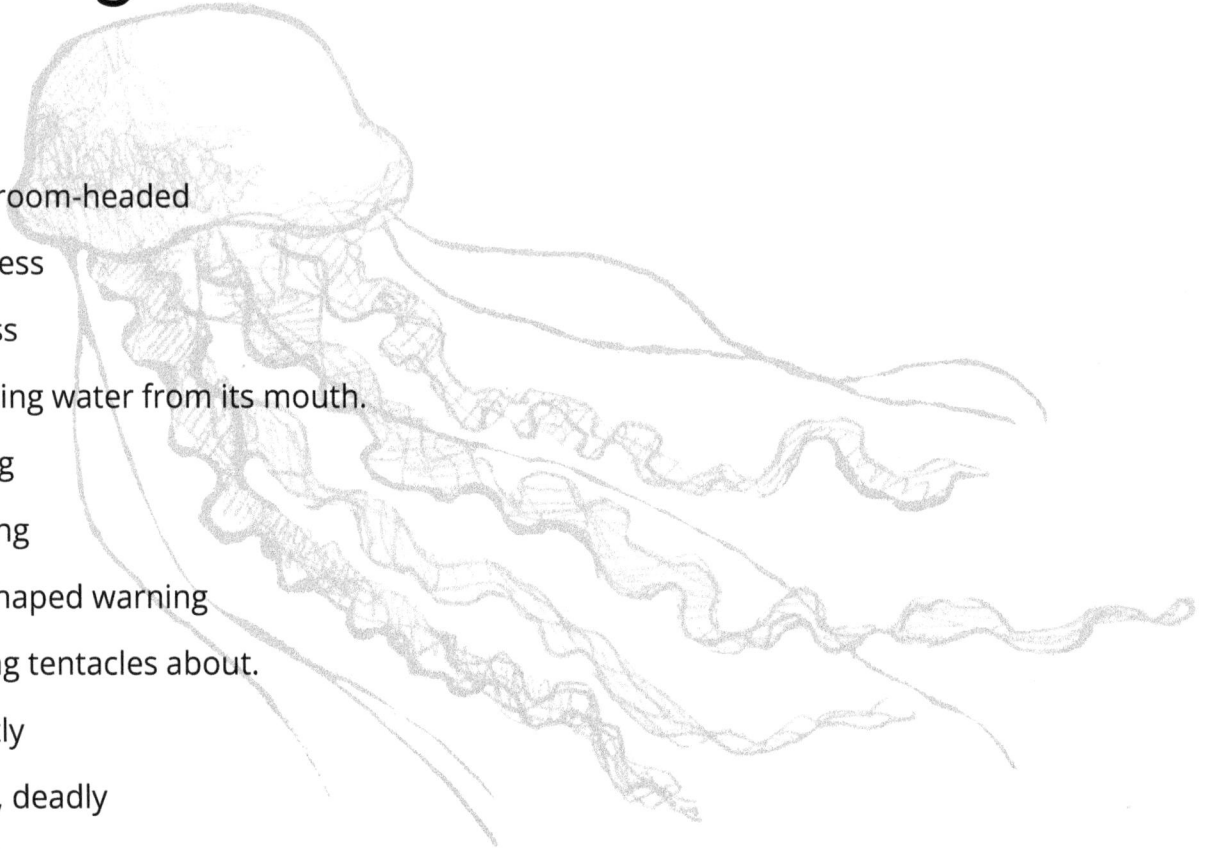

Fun Fact

Jellyfish have been around since before the dinosaurs. For a "fish" without a backbone, that's one tough jelly.

Sea Turtle

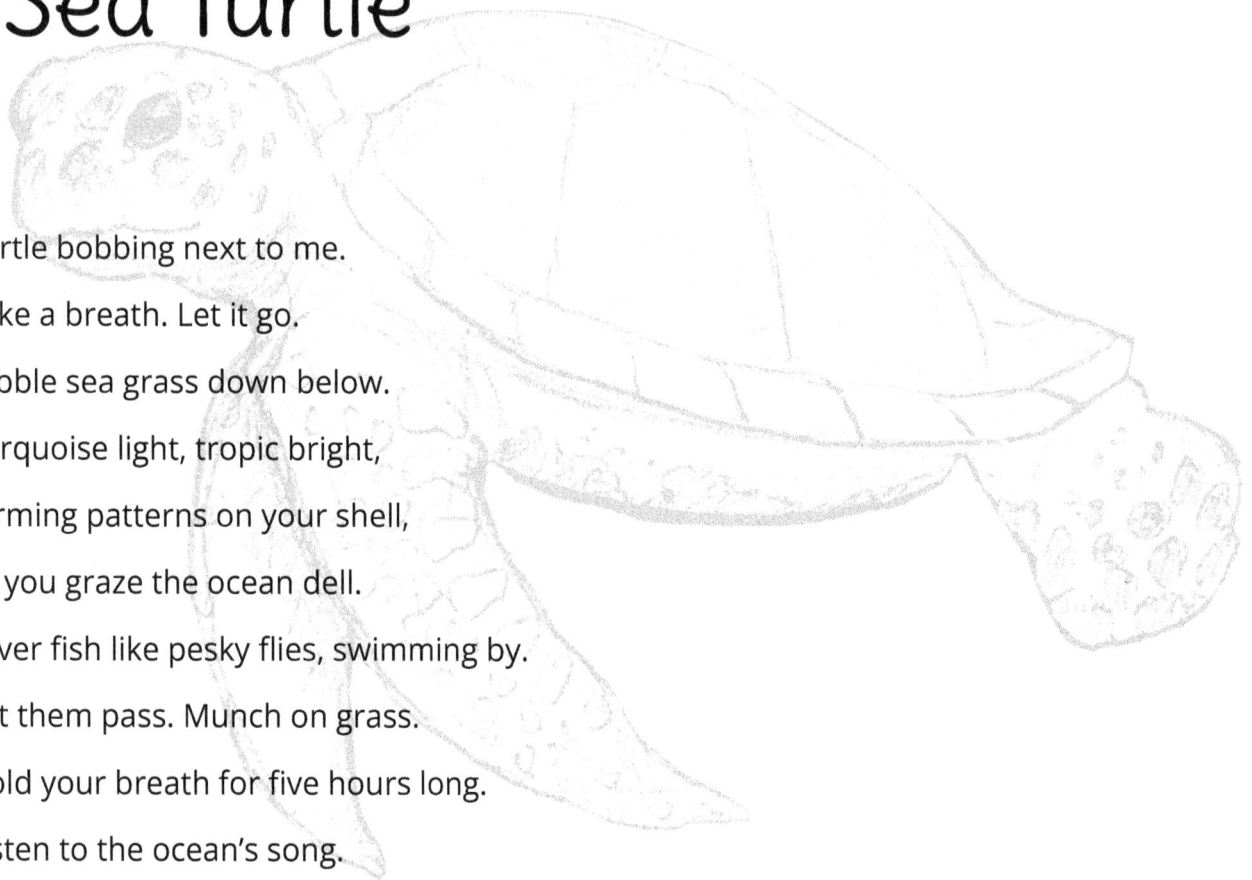

Turtle bobbing next to me.

Take a breath. Let it go.

Nibble sea grass down below.

Turquoise light, tropic bright,

forming patterns on your shell,

as you graze the ocean dell.

Silver fish like pesky flies, swimming by.

Let them pass. Munch on grass.

Hold your breath for five hours long.

Listen to the ocean's song.

Fight the tide, ocean ride.

Poke your head above the sea,

swimming right there next to me.

Test the breeze and take a look.

For a moment we both stare.

You don't care. Suck in air.

Tilt your shell to dive back down,

touching light on sandy ground.

Disappearing 'neath the waves,

graceful as a rocking boat,

happy grounded or afloat.

Fun Fact

The temperature of the eggs in the nest determines if the turtle will be female or male.

Stoplight Parrotfish

Parrotfish wears red and black,
gleaming scales across his back
but only when a juvenile.

Green and gold are more his style,
as from small to XL size,
he keeps growing till he dies.

Fun Fact

Parrotfish can change gender from female to male. Their colors change as gender changes.

Nurse Shark

On ocean's floor

this carnivore

roams in search of herring—

A fisherman

that's quick to catch

but not too fond of sharing.

Fun Fact

Nurse sharks sometimes "walk" or "roam" along the ocean floor using their pectoral fins.

Sting Ray

With rapier tail and beady eyes,

you look like a caped crusader

who glides through sands in a watery home,

hiding from all invaders.

When ocean currents wash past you,

you seem to be waving a greeting.

Perhaps a hello from the shallows below

bodes well for a friendly meeting.

But I think I'll stay on the surface,

though gentle and harmless you are.

Creatures with sword-like features

I'd rather observe from afar.

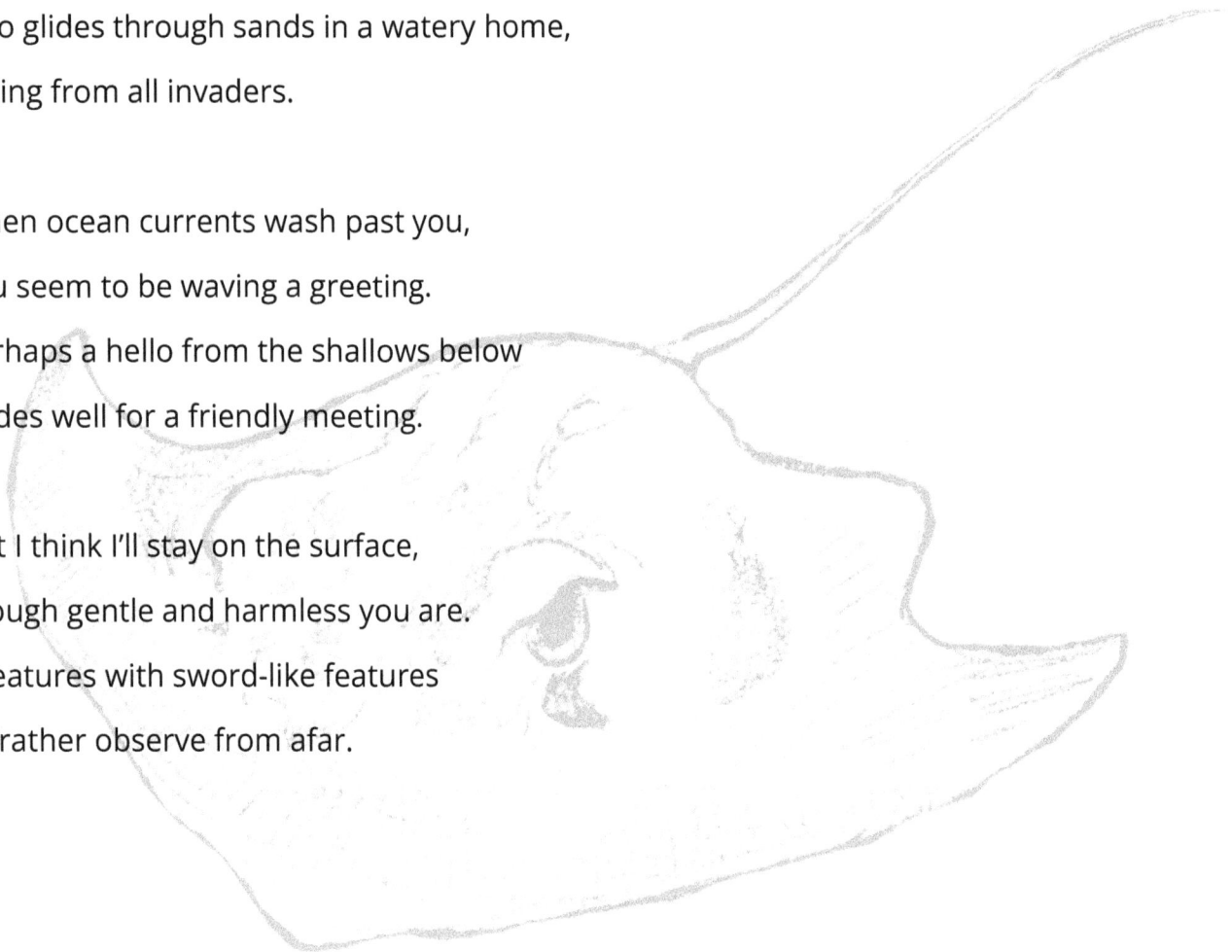

Fun Fact

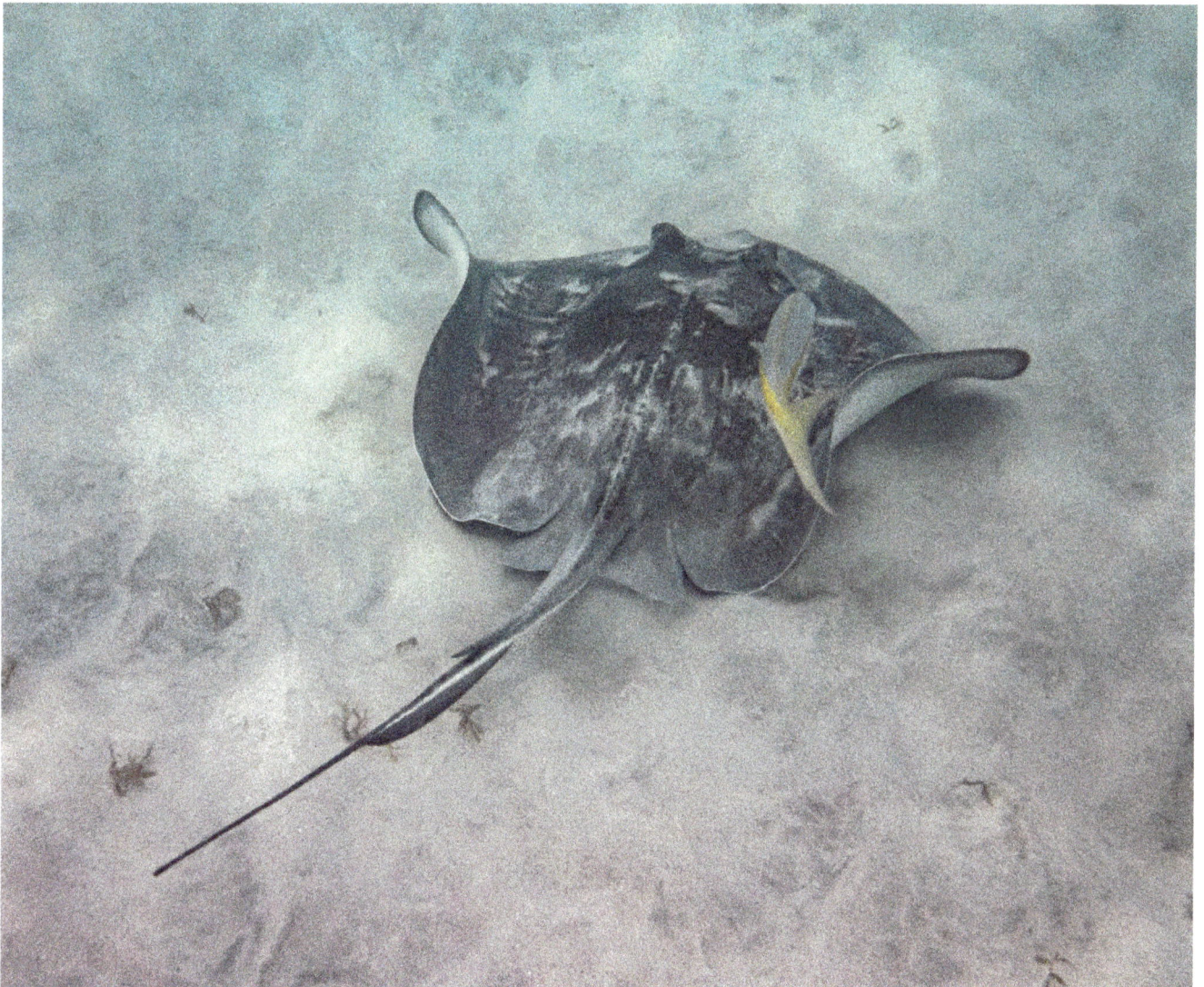

Sting rays are non-aggressive and spend most of their time hiding in the sand. Divers shuffle their feet when walking in shallows to avoid stepping on them.

Hermit Crab

In his house made of shell
hollow coils hide him well.
Hermit's home on his back
as he moves down the track.
Gone to scavenge in the sea,
make a friend—anemone.

Tides collect, push to shore
seashell treasures—homes galore.
He will search with stalky eyes
for a house of bigger size,
find another place to dwell—
someone else's empty shell.

Fun Fact

Some hermit crabs can carry anemones on their backs. The anemone may even stay with its partner when he changes shells.

Squid

Mother lived on the coral reef,
but I like open sea plains.
I hide within the turtle grass
through brief Caribbean rains.

Tucked beneath the ebbing tide,
I peer through turquoise depths.
My three hearts thrum. My big eyes blink.
My eight arms paddle west.

From isle to isle I flit about,
hunt shrimp at ocean's rim,
If sharks are out, I use my skills—
squirt jets of ink at them.

Fun Fact

Squids sometimes communicate by changing their skin pigments. They flash color patterns to talk to each other.

Puddingwife Wrasse

Silver sides, stripes of blue,

beauty queen, that's me.

Bronze eye makeup, brushy fins,

shy personality.

Though I dazzle, solitary

is my status quo.

Others say I'm pretty. Still,

I swim the seas alone.

Fun Fact

Puddingwife Wrasses are first to bed and last to rise, likely because of their shy natures rather than because they are sleepy.

Spotted Trunkfish

A triangular tank,

with plated scale armor,

the trunkfish seems like

it'd be hard to harm her,

but she's not so large.

Her face isn't scary—

with lips pursed for kissing,

it's hard to be wary.

A black-spotted body

in gold-finned gown—

she's less like a warrior

and more like a clown.

Fun Fact

Trunkfish release a colorless poison when touched. They use this defense against predators such as the nurse shark, which can die if it ingests the toxin.

Four-eyed Butterfly Fish

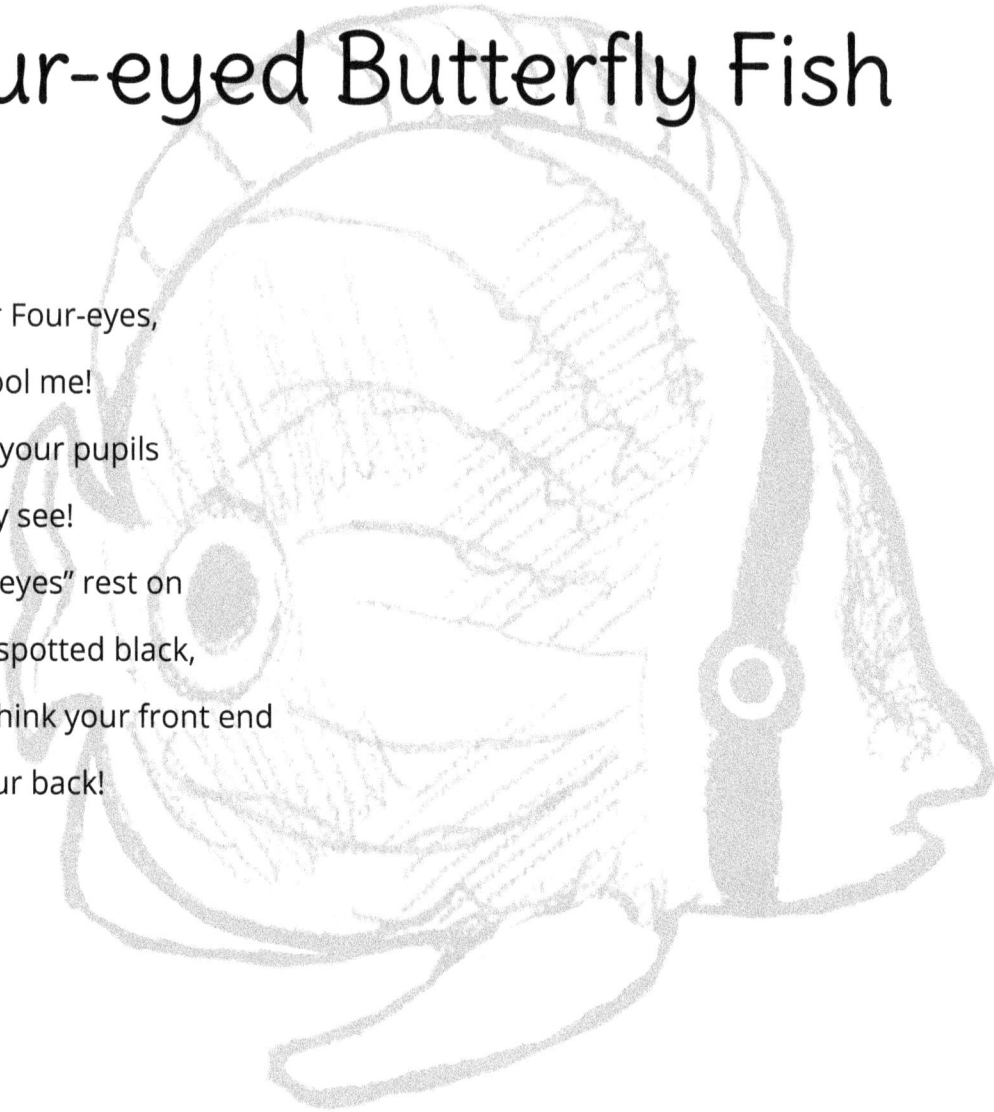

Hey, Mister Four-eyes,

you can't fool me!

Just two of your pupils

can actually see!

The other "eyes" rest on

your sides spotted black,

so sharks think your front end

is really your back!

Fun Fact

There are over 130 kinds of butterfly fish. As coral reefs shrink, so does the number of butterfly fish, which feed on crunchy coral.

Blue Tang Fish

Near Davy Jones' Locker
in the deep blue sea,
a school of blue tang fish
sweep past me.

Shivering their gills
as water runs through,
wiggling their fins
as they bid adieu.

Sticking close together
like a gang of toughs,
navigating coral
in the ocean roughs.

Crew without a captain,
pirates dressed in blue,
but cuter than the swabbies
in old Blackbeard's crew.

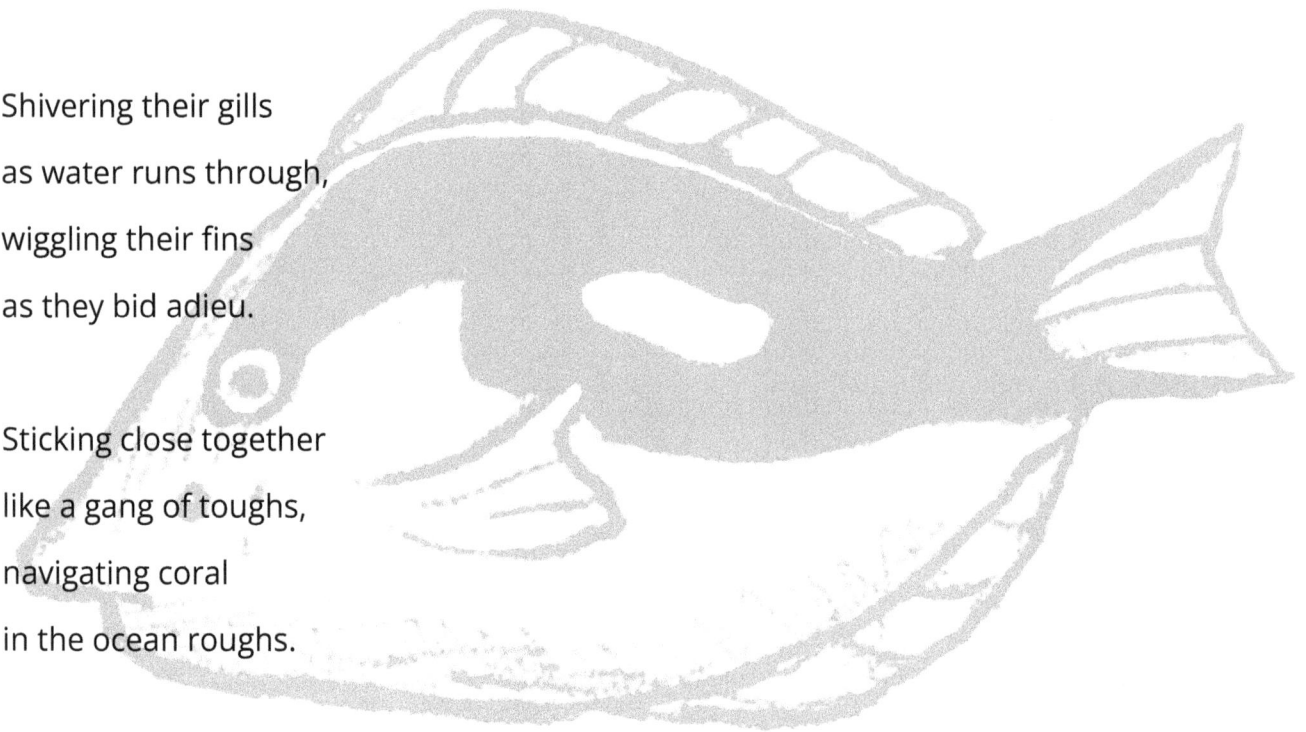

Fun Fact

Blue Tang, like Dory in the movie Finding Nemo, look cute, but they can hurt enemies by thrashing tails tipped with poison spines.

Sea Urchin

Some call me ocean's hedgehog

because of my prickly spines.

Perched on a coral reef,

I'm certainly easy to find.

I grub for algae to eat there.

I'm truthfully not at all picky.

A mussel or fish, even if dead,

I don't find the least bit icky.

I don't mean to poke or hurt you.

I'm really quite harmless to pet.

My tube-like feet will cling to you.

I've never bit anyone yet.

I decorate all five oceans

in hundreds of different designs.

You'll find lots of me, no matter the sea,

and recognize me by my spines.

Fun Fact

Sea urchins are also called "sea hedgehogs." Sea urchins don't have brains, but they have mouths on their undersides.

Schoolmaster Snapper

I'm called "schoolmaster,"

"dogtooth," too,

thanks to huge front teeth.

Fishermen like

the taste of me, so

I hide within the reef.

"Too pretty to eat!"

I'd like to tell

those anglers from above.

But they don't care

about my stripes.

What's under is what they love.

Fun Fact

This snapper has a pair of huge upper teeth that stick out when the fish shuts its mouth.

Barracuda

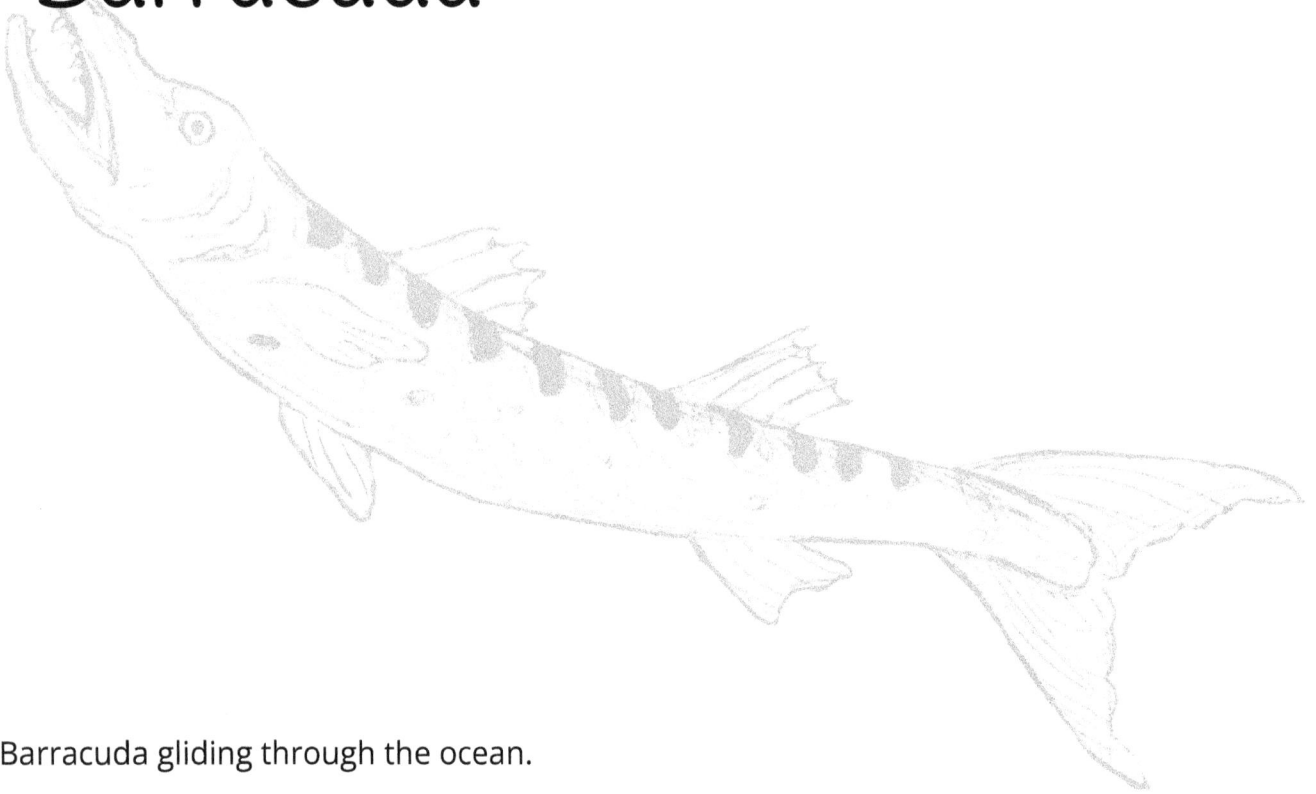

Barracuda gliding through the ocean.

Barracuda swimming through the sea.

Barracuda looking for his dinner.

Hope he doesn't take a bite of me!

Fun Fact

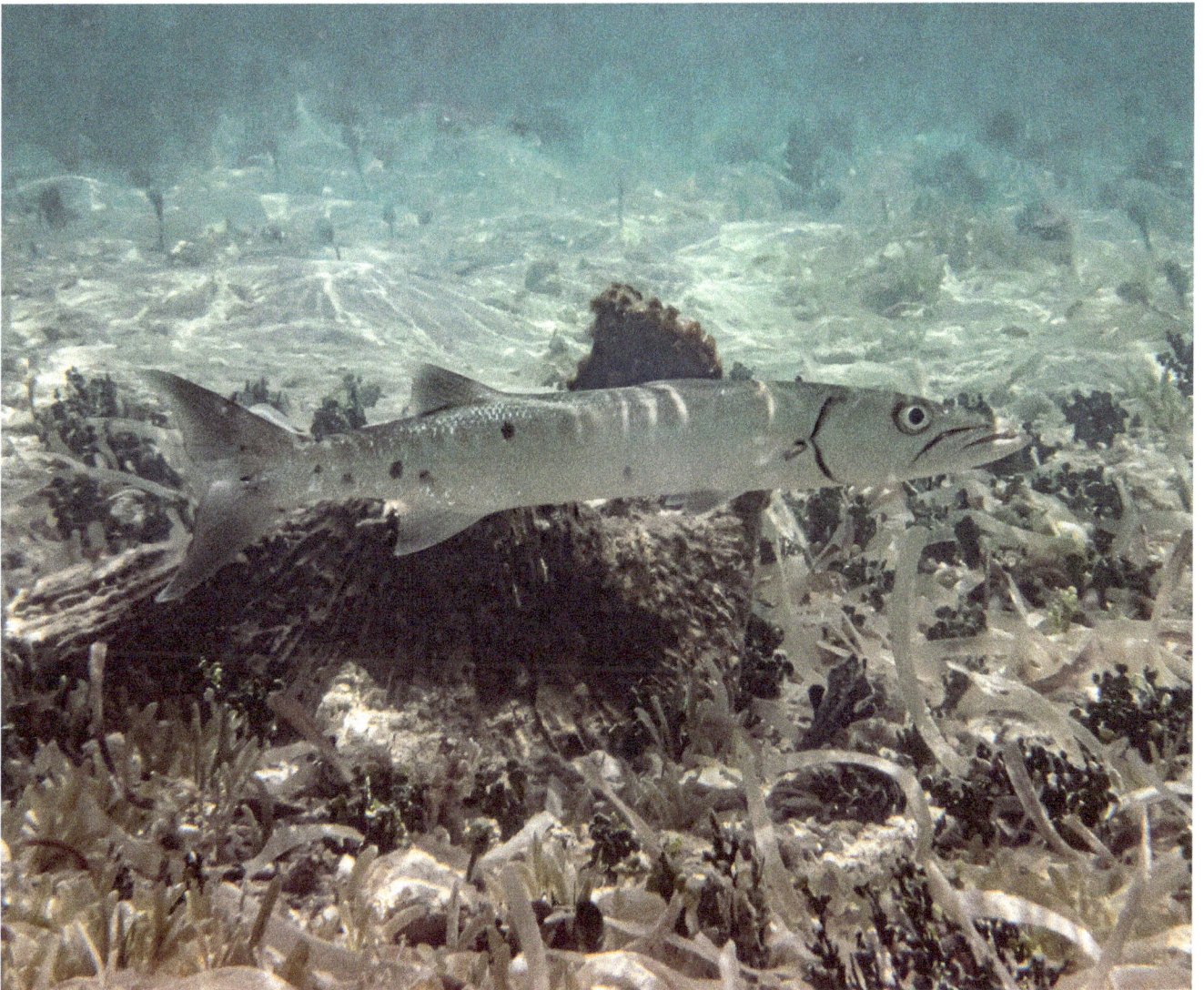

Barracudas use their sight, not smell, to hunt. They are drawn to shiny objects and may accidentally attack humans who enter the water wearing watches or jewelry.

French Grunt

Blue-striped and yellow—

a beautiful fellow.

He grinds teeth to "grunt"—

scares sharks off the hunt.

Fun Fact

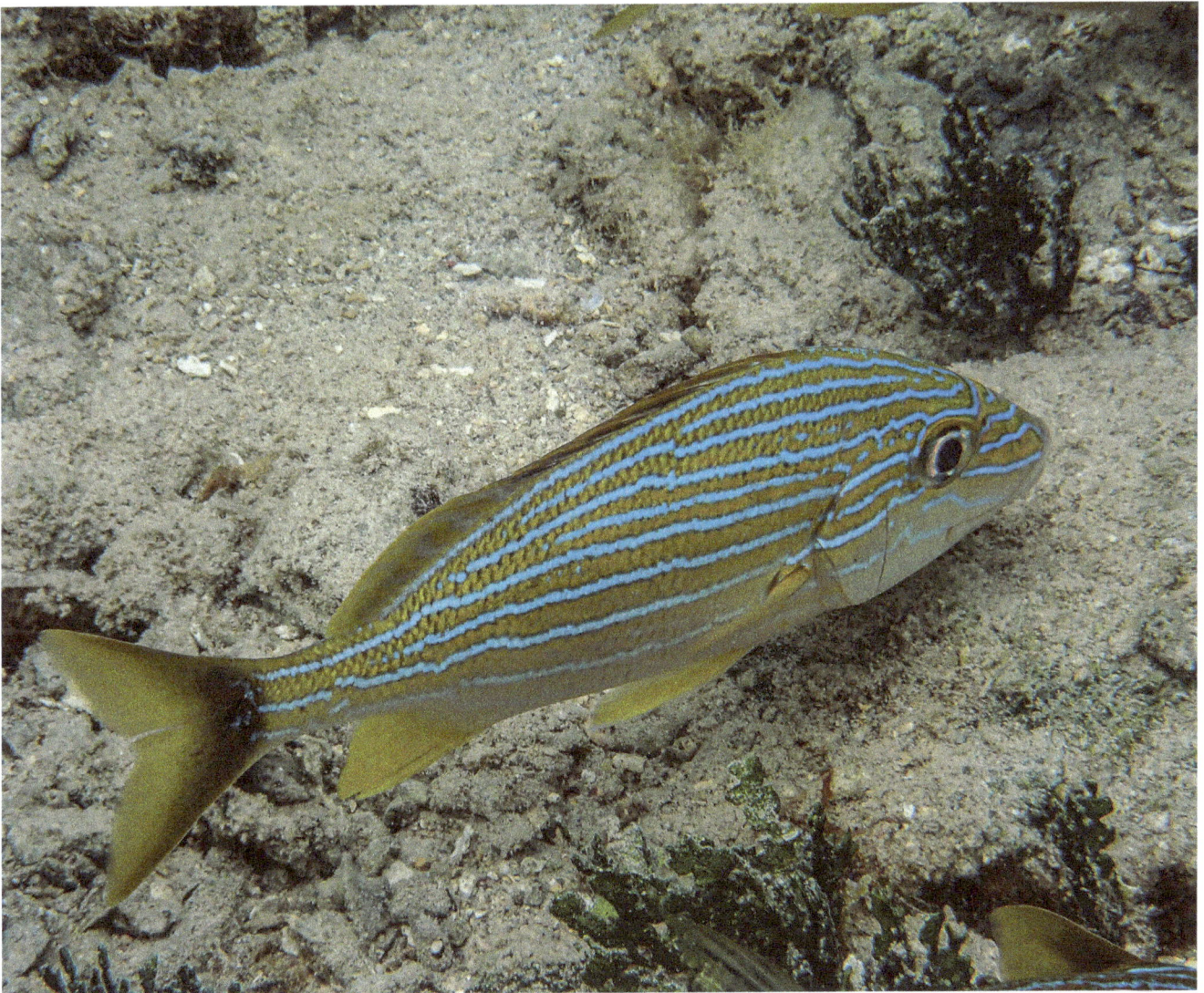

Grunts grind pharyngeal teeth against each other to create grunting sounds. These noises are used to scare predators away.

Bar Jack

"Bar Jack" has a name that sounds

like he's in Blackbeard's pack—

sneaking through a pirate ship

in search of herring snacks.

Fun Fact

There are many kinds of "jack" fish, including the crevalle, yellow, amber, blue runner, leather, and black jack fish.

Coral

I stand in place,

though not a plant.

Be careful not to touch me.

I'm sharp, yet fragile,

radiant, old,

and grow so very slowly.

I love the sun

but live beneath

the salty southern seas.

My family shrinks.

I may not last.

There are no guarantees.

I shelter you

and fishes, too,

from predators and weather.

If I'm to live

and thrive and grow,

we'll need to work together.

Fun Fact

One-fourth of all sea animals live in coral reefs, and half a billion people count on coral reefs for food. They are the "rainforests" of the sea.

Author's Note on Coral Reefs

Like rain forests, coral reefs serve unique and important functions in our world. Coral is a living animal. Coral reefs are made of polyps. Groups of polyps band together and form hard limestone skeletons. The polyps eat algae, which colors them in bright and various rainbow shades. In return, the coral shelters the algae. This is called a symbiotic relationship.

Coral reefs only cover 1% of the ocean floor but provide for 25% of the ocean's sea life. They also slow down waves crashing toward shore. This protects coastlines and the millions of people who live along them. Medicines can be harvested from chemical compounds found in coral reefs. Some reef remnants are millions of years old and can help scientists learn about the distant past before humans arrived. Finally, corals eat small particles that can cloud up the water. That's why waters around coral reefs are so clear.

Today, coral reefs are in trouble. Rising carbon dioxide levels are making the water acidify. Overfishing and warming oceans have put stress on the reef biome. Some colorful reefs have experienced "bleaching," which happens when algae vanish. Without algae, the coral turns white and eventually dies. Plastic litter in the oceans also hurts the fish that dwell there and upsets the reef's balance.

What can you do to help? If you ever visit coral reefs, don't litter, use reef-safe sun lotions and shampoos, and don't touch the coral. You can donate money to help save the coral reefs. Between 2008-2019, more than 14% of the world's coral reefs were lost, and by 2030, most will face critical threats.

Here are some good places to donate:

preserve.nature.org   coral.org   oceanconservancy.org

Bibliography

"Barracudas." *SeaWorld Parks and Entertainment*, seaworld.org. Accessed 5 Mar. 2022.

"Blue Tang." *National Geographic*, nationalgeographic.com. Accessed 10 Feb. 2022.

Cardwell, J.R., and N.R. Liley. "Hormonal Control of Sex and Color Change in the Stoplight Parrotfish, Sparisoma Viride." *General and Comparative Endocrinology*, Jan. 1991, pubmed.gov.

"Cephalopods." *The Animal Communication Project*, acp.eugraph.com. Accessed 15 Feb. 2022.

Champion, Neil. *Caring for the Planet: Seas and Oceans*. North Mankato: Smart Apple Media, 2007.

Debczak, Michele. "Ten Stunning Facts About Stingrays." *Mental Floss*, 15 Aug. 2015, mentalfloss.com.

"The Feistiest of Reef Fish, Damselfish." *Reef Briefs*, ambergriscaye.com. Accessed 23 Jan. 2022.

"Fish Grind Teeth to Grunt." *Nature*, vol. 515, no. 10, 2014, https://doi.org/10.1038/515010a.

"Fun Jack Fish Facts for Kids." *Kidadl*, 6 Aug. 2021, kidadl.com.

"Fun Spotted Trunkfish Facts for Kids." *Kidadl*, 6 Aug. 2021, kidadl.com.

Hoseck, Nicky. "Are Shark Attacks in Costa Rica Common?"." *Dutch Shark Society*, 7 Apr. 2022, dutchsharksociety.org.

Kazilek, C. J. "Urchin Anatomy." *ASU - Ask A Biologist*, 22 Aug. 2015, askabiologist.asu.edu.

McKenzie, Precious. *Coral Reefs*. North Mankato: Rourke Publishing, 2020.

Magloff, Lisa. *Turtle*. New York: Dorling Kindersley Limited, 2007.

Notice, Tashmar. "Halichoeres Radiatus (Puddingwife Wrasse)." *The Online Guide to the Animals of Trinidad and Tobago*, 2016, sta.uwi.edu.

"Tarpon Facts." *Florida Fish and Wildlife Conservation Commission*, myfwc.com. Accessed 2 Feb. 2022.

Vigil, Sandy. "Relationship Between Hermit Crabs and Sea Anemone." *Pets on Mom.Com*, animals.mom.com. Accessed 14 Mar. 2022.

Wearing, Judy. *Jellyfish*. New York: Weigl Publishers, Inc., 2010.

Woodard, Colin. *The Real Pirates of the Caribbean*. Boston: New Word City, 2014.

Acknowledgements

Thanks to Jean Helmer, Michelle Morin, Holly Moseley, and Cody Mills for their invaluable advice.

Also, thanks to Rick and Kelly Stefanich, for inviting us along with them to explore the islands of St. Thomas and St. John, where most of these photos were taken.

And a very special, HUGE thank you to Kaya Glasner, our talented illustrator and art major at the University of Arizona.

About the Author, Photographer, and Illustrator

Meet the Author

Kathy Bjornestad is a retired K-12 school librarian and Language Arts teacher. She has been writing novels since the fifth grade and has experimented with poetry, novels for all ages, and creative nonfiction. Bjornestad is an award-winning author who calls the Black Hills of South Dakota home. She believes in the power of books to promote empathy and awaken wonder and appreciation for the natural world.

Meet the Photographer

Heidi Stefanich is an Early Literacy teacher, award-winning photographer and full-time nature geek living in the Black Hills of Wyoming. She has been fascinated with photography since she built a pinhole camera for a science fair as a middle-schooler, and is especially excited to contribute to this book in an effort to promote both rhyming (a critical building block for future reading success) and an interest and awareness of the natural world around us.

Meet the Illustrator

Kaya Glasner is an artist based in southern Arizona. She is part of the Illustration, Design & Animation Program at the University of Arizona. Kaya specializes in murals, book illustration & character animation. Her animation and set-building work have been shown twice at The Loft Cinema in Tucson. For more information, visit https://www.professionalscribblesbykaya.com, or contact professionalscribblesbykaya@gmail.com.

www.ingramcontent.com/pod-product-compliance
Lightning Source LLC
Chambersburg PA
CBHW041611260326
41914CB00012B/1458